The Top Ten Myths
of
Enlightenment

Exposing The Truth About Spiritual Enlightenment That Will Set You Free!

The Top Ten Myths
of
Enlightenment

*Exposing The Truth About
Spiritual Enlightenment That Will
Set You Free!*

S. F. Howe

Diamond Star Press
Los Angeles

The Top Ten Myths of Enlightenment: Exposing The Truth About Spiritual Enlightenment That Will Set You Free!

Copyright © 2018 S. F. Howe

Published by Diamond Star Press
Trade Paperback: First Edition
ISBN 13: 9780977433575
ISBN 10: 0977433579

Books by S. F. Howe

Matrix Man
How To Become Enlightened, Happy And Free In An Illusion World

The Top Ten Myths Of Enlightenment
Exposing The Truth About Spiritual Enlighten-ment That Will Set You Free!

The Bringer
Waking Up To The Mind Control Programs Of The Matrix Reality

Secrets Of The Plant Whisperer
How To Care For, Connect, And Communicate With Your House Plants

Your Plant Speaks!
How To Use Your Houseplant As A Therapist
Coming Soon!

Vision Board Success
How To Get Everything You Want With Vision Boards

Sex Yoga
The 7 Easy Steps To A Mind-Blowing Kundalini Awakening!

Transgender America
Spirit, Identity And The Emergence Of The Third
Gender

Morning Routine For Night Owls
How To Supercharge Your Day With A Gentle Yet
Powerful Morning Routine!

When Nothing Else Works
How To Cure Your Lower Back Pain Fast!

Free Gift

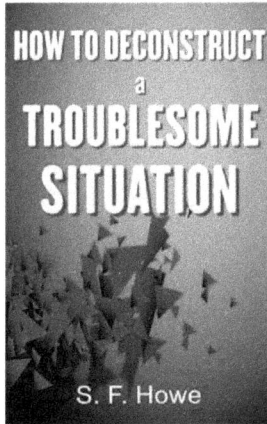

As our thanks to you for reading *The Top Ten Myths Of Enlightenment: Exposing The Truth About Spiritual Enlightenment That Will Set You Free!*, we would like you to download the bonus report, "How to Deconstruct a Troublesome Situation." Inside this report is a powerful technique that will help you strip any problem down to its core and give you the objectivity needed to find the best solution. To get your bonus gift, go to https://bit.ly/DeconstructSituation/

For all spiritual seekers,
that you may be safe on your journey.

Table of Contents

Author's Preface

Let It Go

Be prepared to have everything you thought to be true about enlightenment upended. Try to relax and allow the information to wash over you without having to automatically reject it and jump to the defense of your closely held beliefs.

One of the hallmarks of enlightenment is an open mind and the release of the need to be "right." This single intractable position (the need to be right) has justified all manner of conflict throughout human history, from the smallest interpersonal disagreements up to and including world wars. World peace would be attained instantly if everyone just gave up the obsessive need to be right.

THE TOP TEN MYTHS OF ENLIGHTENMENT

The need to be right arises from an animal level state of consciousness steeped in the primal fear of death and the instinct to survive at all costs. But we are not animals and we live in the modern world where ideas and writings are abundant, and many hold beliefs different from ours.

We are just talking ideas here: your survival is not at risk. You are safe, so take a deep breath and go with it. In these writings, you may discover a voice that says what many think but few dare to express.

Introduction

What Is Enlightenment?

No word triggers more controversy than 'enlightenment,' yet everyone thinks they know what it means—a perfect state of being—and what it looks like—an Indian man in a white robe, with a staff and long white beard.

Most people assume they themselves are not enlightened, that it is something they would have to work very hard for a very long time to achieve, that the likelihood of success is comparable to winning the lottery, and that everybody else they know, other than certain Indian gurus, is not enlightened either, nor could they possibly, short of a miracle, ever be.

THE TOP TEN MYTHS OF ENLIGHTENMENT

Without realizing it, many Westerners view enlightenment in establishment terms derived from mainstream sports, medicine, government, media, education, religion, military and business. Here are the top ten commonly held Western beliefs about what you must do and what you must be to become enlightened.

First: Enlightenment is a secret mission you are on, something you must seek until you find.

Second: Enlightenment can someday be achieved if only you have enough commitment, study and practice.

Third: You need to isolate yourself from the world in order to become enlightened.

Fourth: To become enlightened, you must find a guru to worship.

Fifth: Enlightenment is the most desirable of all goals.

Sixth: The enlightened one is always blissed out.

Seventh: You must maintain an array of daily, enlightenment-inducing mind and body practices.

Eighth: You must leave behind your past and adopt a new appearance and an enlightened name.

Ninth: The enlightened one is loving and kind, never angry and always serene.

Tenth, my personal favorite: The enlightened one has special powers and his life is perfect.

False beliefs about enlightenment go on and on, creating a nearly impenetrable barrier to understanding what enlightenment really is. Without this understanding, many seekers spend a lifetime on the road to a dead end, consoling themselves with the illusion of "spiritual growth" or whatever silver lining they can conjure up.

Interestingly, every myth of enlightenment can be turned inside out and viewed from multiple perspectives. Each myth usually has at least one equal and opposite myth, both of which need to be debunked.

So many myths accompany the concept of enlightenment, that in order to comprehend what enlightenment really is, we first need to understand what it is not. In the following ten chapters,

we will explore the top ten myths of enlightenment.

By the end of this book, you will have
expanded your understanding of what it takes to
become enlightened, what it looks like in practice
and how it affects your life. You will discover that
enlightenment is only a thought away for those
who resonate to its call.

Myth #1

Seek And You Shall Find

The idea that we need to seek enlightenment, as if it were a goal that can be pursued, like a fox by a hound, is the first big myth of enlightenment. In truth, there is no seeking required or involved in enlightenment. Seeking will not bring about enlightenment.

The only thing you accomplish by seeking is more seeking, for what you focus on increases. If you do find something, it will be a projection of your own expectations based on your level of consciousness.

Enlightenment is not a pursuit, not a game, and certainly not a goal. Even though gurus invariably encourage the romancing of enlightenment, they are not admitting the truth to their followers and, perhaps, not even to themselves.

Enlightened people are born for enlightenment. They did not create it in themselves, nor did any other person, such as a guru, create it in them.

Most seekers fail to understand that every persona that appears in the illusion world is assigned a bandwidth of awareness by their higher self (i.e., Source consciousness). Each persona's bandwidth contains a lower to higher range of frequencies. The lowest range of the bandwidth represents the lowest frequency that persona is designed to access. The top of the bandwidth is the maximum allotted consciousness possible during the run of that persona's story.

A bandwidth exists for every stage of consciousness in the human population. However, it works like a bell curve, with a smaller percentage of people at the bottom left, inhabiting a near animal level consciousness, to the mid-range of the bell, which is the conventional consciousness of the vast majority, to the smaller percentage on the far right which signals varying levels of advanced consciousness all the way up to enlightenment and beyond.

In other words, even characters in the advanced levels of the illusion cannot become self-realized just because they want to, or because they have meditated long and hard, took ayahausca with the best Amazon shaman, or received vibrational boosts and visions of the higher worlds from their guru. Nor can personas in low or mid-level bandwidths suddenly awaken to an advanced level of consciousness.

If and when enlightenment does come, it is only possible for the ones in the most advanced levels because a) it is part of their story and b) within the range of their bandwidth.

While all bandwidths have range, the range is actually quite small. It permits some movement or potential up and down within the consciousness of the persona in that bandwidth, but it does not allow for unlimited expansion or unlimited contraction.

You cannot force or manipulate enlightenment. Enlightenment happens to you, and often it happens without any preparation whatsoever. All the preparation in the world cannot make enlightenment happen to you if it is not part of your story. If you appear to have sought and found enlightenment, then enlightenment was in the design for your story.

That said, we are not suggesting that you change anything about what you are doing if you are in fact actively seeking enlightenment. You will do what you must do. If you feel called to pursue enlightenment, then, by all means, do so, as that is your story and your path. You will inevitably learn and experience much in the traversing of your path.

The purpose of this chapter is to help you understand that each persona has a pre-assigned bandwidth of consciousness and that there is no cause to judge another person's level of consciousness, or your own for that matter.

All That Is explores itself through every variety of experience and every level and state of awareness. It created the lower levels, the mid levels, the higher levels, and everything in between, for its own intents and purposes.

When you truly grasp the truth of this, you automatically accept where you are and where others are. In so doing, you are well on your way to enlightenment as compared to the average person.

For an in-depth exploration of how our illusion world operates, please visit Amazon.com and check out my foundational work, *Matrix Man: How To Become Enlightened, Happy & Free In An Illusion World.*

Myth #2

Enlightenment Is An Achievement

For the spiritual high achievers, enlightenment is a worthy goal, not unlike a mountaineer's dream to conquer Everest. If only enlightenment could be achieved like any other goal.

For example, in attempting to lose weight, if a method is chosen and consistent effort, intention, commitment and practice are applied, the result is fairly certain. However, with enlightenment, you are achieving a state of being which not only cannot be quantified, but also which the pursuit of, like the legendary Tasmanian Tiger, is most likely to cause it to remain firmly outside of your grasp,

Enlightenment cannot be chosen; it chooses you. The method you attribute to your breakthrough is another person's dead end. There can be no deliberate pursuit of the target because the target is both difficult to define and always moving.

There are as many definitions of enlightenment as there are seekers. However, the actual experience is something that can never be imagined before it happens. Not only is it unimaginable to your current consciousness, it is impossible to recognize as having occurred in another person unless you are in that same state of consciousness.

We see what we know, and when we look at a guru and call him enlightened, we are really just expressing our ignorance of what enlightenment looks like. In fact, most gurus are playing a traditional role around which there is much lore, a role that they are naturally good at. Their job is to fill a need in the lives of their followers, that is, to fulfill their disciples' ideas of what enlightenment looks like.

Their followers need to think they are seeing something beyond themselves, something wise, ideal and magical that they can aspire to. This keeps them focused on the goal of enlightenment and passionately engaged in their spiritual practice. In order to persist in this pursuit, they must remain in denial of their own wisdom, awareness and holiness by unconsciously projecting it onto the guru before them. He is simply a mirror that reflects their unconscious expectations back to them.

As a result of their belief in the guru's holiness, which is accompanied by the literal projection of their psychic energy into the guru, the spiritual leader is sustained and energetically fed by his devotees' reverence, devotion and financial support.

Filled with the energy of their projections, the guru is empowered to feed back to his flock what they need to hear. The flock empowers the guru, literally and figuratively, but always remains one down in a position of worship of the guru based on their belief that he is enlightened and they are not. Followers rarely, if ever, contemplate the idea that it is all theater, that the guru-persona is what someone looks like who is portraying an unenlightened persona's idea of enlightenment and is not far removed from the childish concept of God as a wise man in the sky with a long white beard..

The abundant historical lore about enlightenment further has the student believing that the enlightened person cannot function in the world and therefore needs the rarified environment of an ashram and the care of his disciples.

It is also common to believe that the guru sacrifices himself for his followers, meaning that he remains with them in order to trigger their enlightenment, rather than chooses this lifestyle for his own reasons. An unsophisticated spiritual student does not know that the truly enlightened rarely announce themselves, nor do they seek followers.

When you finally realize that you cannot achieve enlightenment through your own practical efforts, much less through your association with a guru, you must accept that if it does come, it will manifest in whatever way your higher self has designed for your life.

Invariably the experience is a big surprise, a radical departure from your previous state of awareness, which is effectively rendered defunct, and you will definitely know if or when this happens.

Myth #3

Enlightenment Requires Isolation

This myth states that in order to become enlightened, a person must isolate themselves from the world, perhaps by living in a cave or monastery. Furthermore, many also believe that, once enlightened, you become immune to lower vibrations. We shall explore both of these myths, which are two sides of the same coin.

Isolation is not a prerequisite for enlightenment because becoming enlightened is determined by your story, not by an external condition. Even though isolation may be the setting for one persona's enlightenment, it doesn't mean there is a rule that states enlightenment requires isolation.

However, because most seekers also believe that, once achieved, enlightenment is like spiritual armor and that a persona can remain enlightened under any and all circumstances, they do not understand that enlightenment is actually delicate—a vibrational frequency which flourishes in a specific kind of existence. Therefore, a degree of isolation *after* enlightenment can be helpful.

The existence that supports enlightenment tends to be free and peaceful, meditative, close to nature, with abundant passive income and a good degree of detachment from worldly obligations. However, please note that such a lifestyle does not necessarily trigger enlightenment. The purpose of such a lifestyle is to sustain enlightenment because it gently supports a higher vibration.

Even enlightened ones need environmental support to maintain the sanctity of their high vibration. The world does not support a high vibration, much less higher dimensional knowledge.

Our planet is in a dark sector, largely entrained to low and dark vibrations, which provides myriad challenges for the enlightened, not to mention for all those who would aspire to enlightenment. Therefore, the enlightened need sanctuary—a protective lifestyle—within which to restore themselves when excessive or unexpected contact with the lower vibrations threatens to overwhelm.

Immediately following enlightenment, a persona who has long been interacting with the system, the mainstream and the conventional will find that all forms begin to drop away. They will most likely not be able to hold that job, continue in that graduate program, relate to their family of origin, or sustain their marriage and friendships. If a complete or near-complete emptying of the forms of that persona's reality has not occurred within two years of the enlightenment event, it was likely not true enlightenment.

If it indeed was true enlightenment, you will find yourself losing or relinquishing everything, literally everything. That is the real effect of a radical shift in consciousness on a persona's life:

total annihilation of the outer structure of your life.

Fortunately, your ecstatic awakening to enlightenment provides an emotional cushion against the hardships—the multiple physical, emotional, social and financial losses—that inevitably follow. Through their joyful perspective, the enlightened ones tend to view these losses as essential change.

Some of those left behind will respond with great animosity to the loss of you and make a hellish drama over what was in fact the result of a vibrational and perceptual shift in your consciousness. Others will sense the shift and come on strong to bring you back into the fold. But once they realize you are untouchable and have mysteriously moved on, they sink into feelings of rejection. The enlightened one must live forever with the bewilderment and festering resentment of those left behind.

If you were not isolated before enlightenment, you will be once enlightenment has occurred. So do not seek the mountaintop, the cave or the monastery. For enlightenment will reduce you to complete aloneness and set you adrift. It will seek you out and strike when you least expect it, when you are just like everyone else, in the midst of the most ordinary and conventional pursuits. In so doing, it severs you from all of your attachments and endeavors until you are completely isolated as if in a cave of your own undoing, no matter that you had never set foot in a cave before.

Myth #4

You Need A Guru

The 2011 documentary "Kumare" is a must-see for enlightenment seekers. It perfectly sums up the myths of enlightenment. In this film, a young, secular Indian-American named Vikram Ghandi, performed a social experiment. He grew his hair and beard long, donned robes and adopted a heavy Indian accent ("like my grandmother's"). Presenting himself as a guru newly arrived from India, he began giving talks and workshops for new age groups in Arizona. Before long he had a devoted following who attributed their association with him, his "practices" and his "wisdom" as having brought them healing and increased awareness. When he finally revealed his deception to his followers, many left in anger, but others remained to embrace him as he really was.

Most spiritual seekers have not had a primal experience of their oneness with Source, much less the realization that their own Awareness of Being is the consciousness of the Absolute. This understanding inures a persona against worshipping another human being because they know that the Supreme resides within All.

Seekers who believe they need a guru have a strong desire to achieve spiritual growth and enlightenment but feel they could never achieve this on their own. Thinking in conventional terms dictated by their culture, as if seeking a piano teacher to learn to play the piano, they have concluded that a teacher, a model, is needed in order to learn how to be enlightened. This belief is strongly reinforced by the philosophical teachings of ancient Asian gurus, which form the basis of most contemporary ideas about enlightenment.

By observing their guru in action, they will somehow integrate higher ways of being. By following the guru's teachings, they will be uplifted and brought closer to enlightenment. By practicing as the guru practices or as he instructs them to practice, they will increase their vibration and the likelihood of achieving enlightenment.

There is always something to be gained by watching a master at work and receiving instruction from a master, especially when learning a skill. But enlightenment is not a skill and this kind of learning does not ensure enlightenment.

Followers of a guru hope that by osmosis they will be infected with the Enlightenment Virus, otherwise known as receiving 'transmissions' from the guru. Transmissions are one of the hallmarks of a guru who happily misleads his followers by making himself the connecting link to higher consciousness rather than revealing the truth: everyone is already connected to consciousness but only some will become enlightened and not through any effort on their part. This common guru tactic is mirrored by priests and ministers in the organized religions who also purport to be bridges to God.

There is little that transpires in an ashram that does not in one way or another hark back to the conventional religious behavior (and misbehavior) within the majority religions. Ironically, many religious observances and protocols, similar to the ones eschewed by those who left their religion of birth to seek enlightenment through association with a guru, can be found within the new spiritual organization.

Gurus, like all religious leaders, have a natural affinity for their role and play it well. Some people are simply good at espousing spiritual philosophy and timeless wisdom, but that does not make them enlightened. This distinction is critical in recognizing the practical truth about most spiritual teachers and leaders. If they were not good at what they do because of natural leanings and abilities, they would have selected a different line of work. But while they may be good at the whole 'spiritual thing,' they are playing a role within the earth game. Enlightenment is something else entirely.

Does the history professor who powerfully teaches the exploits of warriors, such as Attila the Hun, make that professor 'the scourge of all lands?' Of course not. Similarly, someone teaching wisdom and truth and behaving in a kind and humble way does not automatically mean they are enlightened.

Myth #5

Enlightenment Is The Most Desirable Goal

While there are no enlightened people who wish for less knowledge and awareness, because one would never choose to go backwards, many would still not recommend the state to others and cannot fathom why it is pursued so passionately.

Most seekers haven't yet realized that enlightenment puts you at the far end of the bell curve, so out of reach of your fellow planetary travelers, you may as well be alone on the planet. Your raised vibration and expanded perspective on reality automatically render most of your previous pastimes, associations, dreams and goals null and void. If ever society seemed crazy to you before, with its sacred cows, immature popular culture and violent media, which the masses addictively consume, it will now reveal itself as stark, raving insanity.

If you wish to lose everything, including your job, home, family, friends and enjoyment of prior pursuits, become enlightened. If you wish to see your loved ones recoil from your heightened perspective and discover the many thoughts and feelings that you can never safely express to them, become enlightened.

If you wish to find the rituals, obligations and practices of your family, religion and culture meaningless and redundant—even the simple things such as celebrating the annual holidays, which bring others comfort and security but feel oppressive to you, permanently designating you an outsider and forcing you to fake it or avoid it— become enlightened.

While most enlightened people do carry on quietly in their lives, no one the wiser, for some, true self-realization triggers an actual spiritual emergency. This simply means that the new perspective on reality is so disorienting, the individual may appear to decompensate into a psychotic state requiring hospitalization. Perhaps the reaction is panic because of the disappearance of the usual sense of self, or perhaps it's a kind of mania brought on by the overwhelming joy that comes from recognizing the truth of who you really are. Alternatively, it may manifest as dropping out and appearing to have lost all motivation whatsoever.

With others in your immediate environment shocked at your changed persona and unable to put a proper name to what you are going through, the culture is happy to declare your awakening to truth as insanity and hospitalize you for it. What follows are psychiatric evaluations and medications, a formal diagnosis, so-called treatment designed to jolt you back to reality, and your eventual release, safely drugged and under the full control of the medical establishment.

In reality, all that happened was that you suddenly woke up with no one to guide you, and you did it a little too noticeably, too dramatically, such that it pulled in the mind controllers of our culture—the police and the psychiatrists—who function as enforcers of the system and whose job it is to make sure you conform as well.

The moral of this story is, if your enlightenment is causing you distress, try to keep it to yourself or seek a spiritual counselor for assistance! Either way, know that you will adjust and that things will settle down in time.

Insofar as the myth of enlightenment as a desirable state to be sought after, consider that the enlightened mind's realigned perspective may be an undesirable development, causing some to react with panic to the unconditioned awareness of being, and others with mania or loss of motivation. Most simply press on, passing as 'regular' but carrying a secret they are unable to discuss with anyone.

So is it desirable to seek enlightenment? Perhaps we were meant to play the earth game all in; not as a watcher of the illusion. In any case, if you are meant to become enlightened, you will be and if not, not.

Myth #6

Enlightened People Are Always Blissed Out

I love this myth. It's true that for the first two years after enlightenment the majority experience prolonged states of bliss and joy. However, that is for approximately, and only, the first two years, during which bliss serves a purpose that goes way beyond the ecstasy of awakening to being the All.

For the first two years after enlightenment, a stripping of all previous roles and attachments occurs. No matter how hard you may try to make your life work during this time, you are released as if by an invisible hand from each and every existing pursuit and attachment. As mentioned before, this may express as a loss of job or, if in school, the urge to drop out, loss of relationships, including spouses, lovers and friends, loss of goals and dreams associated with the aforementioned jobs, school and relationships, and even perhaps, loss of health—mental or physical.

However, this stripping away, this relinquishing of all that defined your previous life, which under normal circumstances would cause incalculable pain, is buffered by your newfound understanding of the nature of reality. The blissed out vibration that possesses you serves as a buffer for the losses that must and do ensue, in much the same way that pain medication dulls suffering after surgery.

One might say that a beneficent and prolonged flood of high vibrations reduces the disorientation entailed in the sloughing off of your previous life. For this you are grateful. There is further a sense of the inevitability of these departures from your life now that you have come into a higher awareness of the true nature of reality.

It may take two years or more to comprehend the full ramifications of having been popped into a higher octave of existence. During that time so much changes that it is important to wait until the ground stops shaking to assess the damage. Once you are stabilized in the new vibration, you may realize that you are still without means, without anyone who can comprehend your new state of being, and without clarity as to your next step. Fortunately, you have trust in the One that lives, moves and breathes as you.

You consecrate your life to God and ask for guidance. That guidance leads you to new circumstances, associates and pursuits. Family members and friends react with concern to your passionate pursuit of goals that may appear to be a drastic departure from your previous trajectory, and are often completely outside the mainstream. How will you survive, they wonder? How will you survive, *you* wonder, hoping your Guide has a plan for that as well. You now embark on a life of meaning, purpose and passion, with none of the security markers that the vast majority cling to.

Your joyful nature fully unleashed carries you through the awkwardness of being a newbie in a new existence. It lifts you above the fears and insecurities that the majority seek to keep at bay at any cost. Into the unknown you choose to walk, step by step, as if creating the road beneath your feet with each step in the direction of your dreams.

And these dreams are no longer the conventional, acceptable and practical dreams you once pursued so successfully. They are the dreams of your soul, of your spirit, of your heart, dreams with wings of power and destinies of fortune. You have come through to the other side and now inhabit a magical existence. You will show everyone what it is to live in trust and love of the Great One that guides you, and in so doing will encourage others to find the truth of their nature and go free.

Wouldn't anyone be high as a kite embarked on such a journey? Bliss is necessary, yes, not only for the soldering of wounds generated by the numerous and repeated losses, but also in order to convince yourself of the purpose and safety in climbing high up into the clouds to follow the greatest dreams you have ever dreamt so that you may weave them into the substance of your everyday life.

This joyful climb, a delirious ascension bursting with meaning, is the reward for giving up the small you. But what is the price for your alignment with the grand Creative Force of the Universe?

It turns out to be a road full of rocks and fissures which appears to oppose your passage at every turn, all the while unfolding smoothly for the masses who revel in the goals, pleasures and pastimes that have been firmly installed through cultural programming, which are never questioned, and which bear a stamp of approval from the system.

With time, your path of challenges devolve into chasms that swallow every ounce of your joy, faith and trust, not once but over and over again, and from which sometimes you feel you may never emerge. And though hope regenerates, it is nevertheless repeatedly sucked from your spirit as you continue to pursue a course which no one understands and at which many secretly jeer.

Your ecstatic path of freedom has become the new slavery. The unconsciousness and enslavement of the masses is still freedom to them.

Such is the path of an enlightened person. Is it nothing but bliss?

Myth #7

Meditate, Pray, Do Yoga, Be A Vegetarian, etc.

Enlightenment does not depend on any of the usual spiritual pursuits of seekers, including meditation, prayer, spiritual study, yoga, vegetarianism or becoming the disciple of an enlightened guru. No matter for how long or how intensely you engage in the ordinary to exotic practices your guru recommends, or which you may have independently adopted for the purpose of enhancing your awareness, opening your chakras, or raising your kundalini, and no matter the energetic changes that may actually result from these practices, enlightenment cannot be bought.

There is a name for the perceptual changes, energy surges and other physical effects of various spiritual practices. It is called 'phenomena.' Phenomena, however, is not enlightenment. It may masquerade as such, convincing you that you have raised your kundalini and activated your crown chakra, or finally opened your third eye, increasing your psychic abilities. But unfortunately, not only are these states temporary, they are not in the final analysis correlated with enlightenment.

Gurus who claim to be enlightened and can demonstrate seemingly magical abilities or unusual physical endurance, are simply utilizing phenomena to enhance their enlightenment cache, but only because they know well the false programming seekers carry around enlightenment, and they aim to make the most of their followers' naiveté.

True enlightenment never happens when you expect it to or in the way you expect it to. It is not something that can be coaxed out of its shell like a turtle, such as by meditating on the I Am for one hour per day, doing deep breathing through one nostril at a time or performing numerous yoga asanas. It is usually so unexpected that the last thing you would have ever imagined happening on that fateful day was *your* enlightenment.

You were perhaps someone who never had thoughts of "spirituality" before in your life. You had likely not studied with a guru or spiritual teacher, much less read the Indian mystics. When enlightenment happens, it floors you. You are forever changed, but in reality your journey has just begun.

So it's not the aliens who walk among us, it's the enlightened ones! (All right, maybe both...) Not to mention that the people around you who already are enlightened are probably the last people on earth you'd ever imagine to be. Why? It is simple—your programming hides the truth from your awareness. You can't see a state of consciousness or recognize a vibration that is higher than your own.

Spiritual gurus, be they mystics of ancient India or spiritual teachers in the present day, are in the business of theatrics. The Holy One ostensibly aims to trigger an awakening to higher consciousness in his disciples by requiring they undertake a wide range of practices, which may include diet, prayer, mantras, meditation, exercise and karma yoga. However, if these gurus were honest they would have to admit how unlikely these physical practices are to ever produce real enlightenment.

Often, gurus have themselves been heavily programmed to associate certain practices with spiritual growth and enlightenment, and are just passing on tired, old belief systems in the guise of enlightened wisdom. Meanwhile, the blatantly unethical spiritual player aims to keep his disciples entirely dependent on him. He is rigorous in requiring the many practices but generous with transmissions, serving himself up as the Source, vibrationally uplifting his followers as long as they remain connected to him, tantalizing them by making enlightenment seem so close, so accessible, but, sadly, always just out of reach.

Enlightenment has nothing to do with so-called spiritual practices. Whereas an advanced level of consciousness is a necessary precursor for enlightenment, it does not also mean enlightenment is something you can pursue as a goal or will even instantly recognize as having happened to you. You will most likely be in shock at having become enlightened, and may not have the words for your new state of being.

To complicate matters, the advanced level encompasses infinite vibrational variations, from lower advanced to the highest level advanced. While the advanced in general tend to be more open to new ideas and aware of the social engineering behind the rituals and obsessions of their culture—their knowing that does not create enlightenment any more than do spiritual practices.

Enlightenment is a gift from the Creative Source which most people will never experience in their story no matter how long or hard they diet, pray, meditate, exercise and perform karma yoga according to the instructions of their favorite spiritual teacher or guru. Nor is it impending and soon to be widespread per new age mythologies of planetary ascension, the pejorative 'shift,' and/or the advent of Indigo children.

New age mythology dies hard, but truth is eternal: enlightenment is a rare state of awareness that only a tiny percentage of people in the illusion world will ever possess.

Myth #8

You Must Leave The Old You Behind

While leaving behind your past, changing your name and adopting a new appearance are common initiation practices demanded by gurus, they have nothing to do with enlightenment. The guru is simply making you his in the guise of ritual. The more distance placed between you and your past life and loved ones the easier it is for him to indoctrinate you into the program. This is usually presented as necessary and for your own highest good because you are entering a new world, embarking on a new beginning, and the old you must be left behind.

The covert purpose of the communal life is to have you give yourself up to the guru on a continual basis so that he can absorb your energy. Gurus cannot maintain their power without followers and, as such, the guru and his followers engage in a symbiotic relationship.

The disciple gives up his power to the guru, thus feeding him energetically, and the guru in turn uplifts the disciple vibrationally, giving him the illusion of spiritual advancement.

Without realizing it, the disciple's higher vibrational state becomes wholly dependent on being in the guru's energy field. If the guru casts someone from the group, that follower will immediately lose their 'high,' meaning the illusion of spiritual growth and all they believed they had achieved, but which was never real.

It is common for a guru to rename a newly arrived seeker, usually with an Indian-style moniker that contains spiritual meaning. In this way, for example, John becomes Satyam, which means 'truth,' and Carol becomes Devi, which means 'divine.'

The ashram has its characteristic clothing styles and colors for men and women, with much spiritual meaning attributed to them. As an example, flowing white may represent purity and surrender, and light blue may signify holiness and order. Alternatively, different colors may represent status in the ashram, similar to freshman, sophomore, junior and senior levels in high school.

The guru's encouragement or demand for you to put distance between yourself and loved ones is usually explained at first as a way to help the seeker more quickly adapt to the ashram and his new spiritual life with the guru. However, its deeper purpose is to isolate the newly arrived disciple in order to more easily reprogram him into the belief system of the ashram. The faster this occurs, the greater the likelihood the new arrival will remain and continue to provide an energy source for the guru.

What is in it for the seeker? He invariably believes that surrendering to this process will lead him to spiritual growth and enlightenment. If this belief were not strongly in place, it would be impossible for an adult man or woman to surrender their freedom and independent thought to an ashram or spiritual commune under the leadership of a guru,

The intense hope, faith, trust and belief in the priceless value they will receive in exchange for surrendering their freedom, avoiding loved ones and adopting a new name and appearance, indicates that such seekers have long ago internalized as true the myths of enlightenment, many of which we are aiming to dispel in this book.

What awaits the freshman disciple is an induction period where he will learn the correct ways of behaving in the ashram and the limits to his freedom of expression. He will learn the ideas, words, moves, practices and adherences required by the guru and his program.

Some of these practices are nothing more than bizarre outgrowths of an awkward and artificial environment, but which have been imbued with great spiritual meaning. In reality, the followers are in denial of their own spiritual power which they have projected onto the guru, who they worship as spiritually powerful and desire to emulate.

If you, dear reader, find yourself already in an ashram or desiring to join an ashram and follow a guru, please do what is in your heart. Each persona walks the path of their story and each story contains the intents and purposes of the higher consciousness that designed it. Perhaps yours is the rare story that is designed to result in enlightenment within this very restricted situation, even though for most, it will not.

While it is not necessary to follow a guru to develop spiritually or become enlightened, for you, dear reader, who feels so strongly to do so, that appears to be exactly what your story requires, though the outcome remains uncertain. Even if it leads to disillusionment and lost years, experience has happened, learning has happened. No matter the outcome, do what you must do and always listen to your own inner voice.

If you should become enlightened in an ashram you will hopefully recognize that this was how *your* story was designed and, therefore, will not use your awakening to create a rule for others to follow, i.e., that you have to be the follower of a guru in an ashram to become enlightened.

Treating events in stories as facts and creating rules based on those stories, is the source of all myths of enlightenment.

Myth #9

Enlightenment Is Freedom From Negativity

A close cousin to Myth #6, which states that an enlightened person is always blissful, is the myth that if you're enlightened you are always loving and free of negative emotions, such as fear, anger, uncertainty and loneliness.

While an in depth exploration of the subject of emotions is beyond the scope of this book, suffice it to say that emotions are defined here as vibrational frequencies that are interpreted and labeled through the filter of cultural programming. As such, the enlightened persona may be said to have access to every shade and gradation of emotion, and to experience the full range of potential of emotion available within the human story. This is the exact opposite of everything you have ever been taught about enlightenment.

If all emotions other than bliss were eradicated with enlightenment, a persona would become a zombie, completely unable to function in this world. But that is so far from the truth.

The enlightened persona is more fully alive than ever before, feeling everything there is to feel and awake to higher knowledge. Some restrictive energy patterns do lift with enlightenment, and a high vibration is the norm bringing with it a propensity for joy and bliss.

While many enlightened people feel a wide range of positive emotions, enlightenment ultimately means true balance, a state of consciousness that is rarely mentioned in the enlightenment or personal development literature.

What is true balance but a place that exists within the gap between light and dark, between positive and negative. It is a state from which a being can consciously choose how to react in a given situation, rather than be controlled by beliefs about or predispositions to the light or dark, the positive or negative.

True balance is the ultimate freedom possessed by the enlightened persona who understands the meaning of polarity; that the light polarity is inseparable from the dark, and that the two trigger one another on a perpetual basis.

To take one's place in the light is to activate an equal and equivalent place in the dark. However, to remain in the gap is to help resolve the eternal war between light and dark.

When it comes to the polarities, the dark energy seeks to control via force for its own selfish purposes. It will usually masquerade as light for as long as its agenda is satisfied. However, if this dissemblance does not bring the desired result, dark will issue force to achieve its end.

Light claims to seek peace, love and freedom, but believes that it knows what is best for others. Therefore, it utilizes heavy judgment and control to help others "see the light."

Neither polarity supports enlightenment although light would have you believe that enlightenment can only occur in the highest vibrations of the light polarity.

However, the truth is that true balance requires a melding of polarities. It utilizes aspects of both polarities to achieve its goals while remaining unattached to any one polarity. It understands how the polarities feed off of one another and perpetuate the ongoing battle between light and dark.

The enlightened person does not limit or avoid the varied emotional palette inherent in living a full and vibrant life. This means that anger *is* felt after enlightenment, as are all the so-called negative emotions, including fear, uncertainty and loneliness.

Enlightened people do not trade their humanity for a steady state of positive energy. They remain open and alive, feeling all there is to feel, thinking all the thoughts that arise, but making better decisions than the average person as a result of those feelings and thoughts.

The enlightened do not judge their feelings, they do not attach to their feelings, nor do they automatically act on their feelings, unlike people of the mainstream who gnaw on their emotions like a bone and love to create drama. Even more important, the enlightened do not attach to their thoughts or allow them to define their existence as do the overwhelming majority of people on this planet.

The enlightened persona has perspective, which gives them pause, which further gives them options, not to mention understanding.

Enlightenment brings with it higher dimensional knowledge and a wisdom that cannot be accessed by the ordinary mind. While this may appear to others as a lack of negative emotions, in truth it is just the natural response to awakening to the true nature of reality in alignment with Source. Along with that comes the recognition of the destructive nature of the polarities and a repositioning of the persona in true balance.

Embodying true balance is an ongoing developmental process that follows enlightenment. It takes time and experience to identify the many ways in which one's previous alignment with one of the polarities affected one's thoughts, emotions, decisions, actions and associations. It further takes time to establish oneself in true balance, and to access the full measure of freedom offered by that vibrational state as it intersects with the ongoing demands of everyday life.

Myth #10

Enlightenment Makes You Perfect

One of the most laughable myths of enlightenment is the idea that enlightenment ensures a perfect life and that an enlightened persona can have anything they want, as if their awakening to truth makes them a favorite of the gods.

Remember the old Buddhist saying: Before enlightenment, chop wood and carry water. After enlightenment, chop wood and carry water.

While it may be said that for some, life after enlightenment continues as before, with the primary change being one of perspective, it is also true that all lives in our realm are governed by entropy. Survival demands, the inexorable passages of life, everyday responsibilities—all of these things persist. There is no escaping the price of living in this illusion world.

That said, if it is part of their story, an enlightened individual may actually experience dramatically enhanced abilities after his awakening. They may discover that the vibrational shift has propelled them into a higher octave of knowledge and creativity.

The discovery and expression of exalted inner resources brings intense joy to the enlightened individual and may awaken dreams that had lain dormant. Native gifts raised to a cosmic level automatically transform the nature of that persona's work.

According to the unique design of their story, the enlightened one may bring forth a work of absolute genius that could not have been conceived earlier, and that in the doing is a perfect expression of their highest potential. But though it may have brought the creator much joy in its creation and though it may contribute something original and valuable to the world, there is no guarantee that the world will welcome it, ignore it, reward it or anything in between.

In fact, it is more likely that the enlightened one will find their most exalted ideas, abilities or accomplishments out of sync with the world—and subject to complete indifference. Thus it becomes a challenge to channel their brilliance into pathways that allow for survival, pathways that may not stretch remotely wide enough to embrace their potential.

Hence, frustration becomes the secret companion of those enlightened ones who exploded into creativity yet whose storyline is designed to keep them in the shadows. Life isn't fair, not even for the enlightened, although their awareness of the true nature of reality buffers them to an extent against the slings and arrows of fortune.

Depending on their unique story, some enlightened ones may be inspired to pursue humanitarian causes in the illusion while others may seek freedom from altruism, idealism or activism. Each one's path is unique, and following one's path from a place of true balance, wherever that may take you, becomes the higher goal for all.

Enlightenment is neither a 'winner takes all,' dear reader, nor a permanent spring break. The enlightened one still carries responsibilities like everyone else—that ever-changing nexus of internal factors and outer circumstances which unceasingly affects how one shows up in the world.

Not every enlightened person develops extraordinary gifts and not every gifted person becomes enlightened; nor are individuals from either camp guaranteed success. For each persona, the story is everything. In serving the story, we fulfill our purpose.

Recognizing that enlightenment does not guarantee worldly success or 'life mastery,' it also does not suddenly turn the enlightened ones into perfect people. Human foibles do not disappear with enlightenment, nor are the enlightened permanently drifting in a sea of bliss without goals or responsibilities, magically receiving support from the universe.

While enlightenment does increase alignment with Source bringing awareness of guidance and synchronicity, it does not remove the need to complete tasks or handle responsibilities in the outer world as required by their story.

Even with the joy and flow that accompanies exalted work, there are tedious tasks that must be completed in everyone's life on a daily basis. Enlightened people have established habits that may either help or hinder them both before and after enlightenment. No matter what, they must still cope with the demands of life like any other persona in the illusion world.

Enlightened people do not suddenly manifest excellent organizational skills whereas before they were completely disorganized. Nor do they instantly stop procrastinating doing the necessary tasks they previously found noxious, much less effortlessly maintain clutter-free desks.

Furthermore, they do not have magical mastery over time thus feeling zero pressure in the face of unavoidable deadlines imposed by the external world. Nor are they likely to find themselves abundantly supported by the universe while not having to lift a finger.

While certain areas of their life may brim over with motivation and inspiration, other aspects of life may be fraught with resistance, manifesting as interpersonal conflict or a lack of will for completing needed tasks even when required for their unique work.

And let us not forget that enlightened personas still have illusion bodies, with nervous systems that feel pain or get stressed, sick or tired just like everyone else, and as such their vibration goes up and down, albeit within the range set by their bandwidth, all day every day.

That said, what enlightenment does bring is the ineffable Awareness of Being accompanied by the joyful Realization of Oneness. As such, the enlightened persona knows the truth of everyone's Being and thus observes the teeming world with compassion while continuing to face the ongoing challenges of their own story.

In Conclusion

Enlightenment Demystified

Thank you, dear reader, for coming with me on this journey. In the previous chapters, I attempted to demystify enlightenment and hopefully assist those of you who are open to these ideas, to make more informed decisions about your own spiritual path.

If, however, some of my statements contradicted your personal truth, triggering intense objections, doubt or even shock, then I also did my job. Beliefs and traditions die hard, and each persona who reads this book will invariably bring to it their own unique perspective and react in their own way.

We are all running individual stories designed by the Essence of our Being for its own intents and purposes. Therefore, reality appears different from every point of awareness in the Whole.

Enlightenment enables one to embrace differences and remain open to new ideas, but it cannot be pursued, romanced, cajoled or forced into existence. However, adopting a practice for deconstructing beliefs helps sustain the mindset of orientation to higher truth, which is an essential precursor to enlightenment.

To that end, I have provided an important bonus chapter entitled "How to Deconstruct a Troublesome Situation." This free report presents a powerful technique for reframing ingrained notions and trying circumstances. Used regularly, it will help deprogram you from the unconscious beliefs that limit clarity and freedom, thus making room for fresh choices and transformational awakenings. To get your free gift, go now to https://bit.ly/DeconstructSituation/

Did You Enjoy This Book?

Dear Reader,

Thank you for reading *The Top Ten Myths Of Enlightenment: Exposing The Truth About Spiritual Enlightenment That Will Set You Free!* I hope you enjoyed this book.

My purpose in writing this book was twofold: to reveal the many false beliefs and teachings on the subject of spiritual enlightenment and to enable my readers to make more informed decisions in their pursuit of spiritual development.

If you would like to recommend this book to other readers, please write a review on Amazon. It will only take a few minutes, and I would appreciate it very much!

Wishing you the very best,

S. F. Howe

Books by S. F. Howe

MIND · BODY · SPIRIT

HIGHER CONSCIOUSNESS

Matrix Man: How To Become Enlightened, Happy And Free In An Illusion World

The author reveals a new reality paradigm that will liberate you from the limiting beliefs and cultural programming that prevent a joyful and fulfilling life. Available in print and digital editions.

The Top Ten Myths Of Enlightenment: Exposing The Truth About Spiritual Enlightenment That Will Set You Free!

Essential reading for spiritual seekers. What no one else will tell you to help you avoid the pitfalls of the spiritual journey. Available in print and digital editions.

The Bringer: Waking Up To The Mind Control Programs Of The Matrix Reality

For those seeking freedom from cultural indoctrination, these channeled teachings offer a higher dimensional perspective on the most ingrained and unquestioned aspects of everyday life, and have the ability to heal and awaken humanity. Available in the digital edition and soon to be available in print.

PLANT INTELLIGENCE

Secrets Of The Plant Whisperer: How To Care For, Connect, And Communicate With Your House Plants

A plant whisperer reveals the hidden truth about plants and why relating to them in a conscious way is vital for their health and well-being. Available in print and digital editions.

Your Plant Speaks!: How To Use Your Houseplant As A Therapist

Let your house plant solve your problems! Discover the little known art of receiving life coaching from your favorite indoor plant.
Coming Soon!

PERSONAL GROWTH

Vision Board Success: How To Get Everything You Want With Vision Boards!

A powerful technique for achieving your goals and manifesting your desires. Available in print and digital editions.

Sex Yoga: The 7 Easy Steps To A Mind-Blowing Kundalini Awakening! i

A technique for activating the chakras to induce a powerful kundalini experience. Available in print and digital editions.

Morning Routine For Night Owls: How To Supercharge Your Day With A Gentle Yet Powerful Morning Routine!

Morning rituals aren't only for morning people, and they don't have to be rough and tumble or performed at top speed to set up a perfect day. Welcome to the world of the gentle yet powerful wake-up routine for night owls! Available in print and digital editions.

CONSCIOUS HEALTH

Transgender America: Spirit, Identity And The Emergence Of The Third Gender

A higher consciousness perspective on the Transgender Agenda; what it is and why it is being rolled out at breakneck speed to socially engineer a gender dysphoria epidemic. Available in print and digital editions.

When Nothing Else Works: How To Cure Your Lower Back Pain Fast!

The simple method that no doctor will ever tell you about. Requires no drugs, no surgery, and no special equipment. Available in print and digital editions.

About the Author

S. F. Howe is a transformational psychologist and noted contributor to the body/mind/spirit literature for books and teachings on the subjects of higher consciousness, personal growth, conscious health and plant intelligence.

Howe began teaching at the university level while a doctoral candidate in clinical psychology, and went on to work in hospitals and clinics for more than 25 years as a psychotherapist, staff psychologist, clinical program consultant and director of chemical dependency and psychiatric programs.

In the midst of graduate studies, a profound spiritual awakening led to a complete reevaluation of the author's life path. Thus began a spiritual journey along the road less traveled, extending far beyond clinical psychology, conventional reality paradigms and both traditional religion and new age spirituality.

While engaged in a unique, ongoing process of discovery, the author enjoys sharing an ever-expanding understanding of the true nature of reality. Howe's primary intention is to bring an end to suffering by guiding others on a well-worn path to truth and expanded awareness.

Many of those who have experienced Howe's input and presence report emotional and physical healing, life-changing realizations and dramatic personal transformation.

S. F. Howe may be contacted for speaking and teaching engagements. Please direct all inquiries to info@diamondstarpress.com.

Free Gift

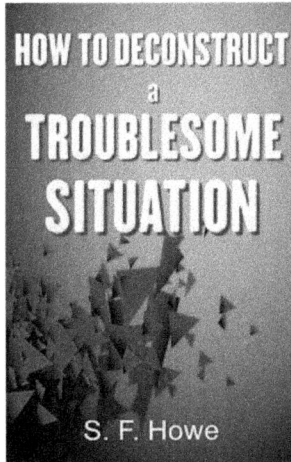

As our thanks to you for reading *The Top Ten Myths Of Enlightenment: Exposing The Truth About Spiritual Enlightenment That Will Set You Free!*, we would like you to download the bonus report, "How to Deconstruct a Troublesome Situation." Inside this report is a powerful technique that will help you strip any problem down to its core and give you the objectivity

needed to find the best solution. To get your
bonus gift, go to **https://bit.ly/DeconstructSituation/**

www.ingramcontent.com/pod-product-compliance
Lightning Source LLC
Chambersburg PA
CBHW062019040426
42447CB00010B/2075